PASSPORT2PURITY® TRAVEL JOURNAL

FamilyLife Publishing®
5800 Ranch Drive
Little Rock, Arkansas 72223
1-800-FL-TODAY • FamilyLife.com
FLTI, d/b/a FamilyLife®, is a ministry of Cru

ISBN: 978-1-60200-521-1

Design: Brand Navigation, LLC

Printed in China

21 20 19 18 17   1 2 3 4 5

FAMILYLIFE®
Help for today. Hope for tomorrow.

Third Edition

PASSPORT2PURITY

P2P

TRAVEL JOURNAL

FamilyLife Publishing®
Little Rock, Arkansas

Contents

WASHINGTON DC
DISTRICT OF COLUMBIA

BEGINNING

1

THE JOURNEY

LAKE

ST JOSEPH AVE

BLUFF RD

ARBORETUM

LAKEVIEW PARK

MAIN ST

Surf SHOP

MADISON ST

BROADWAY ST

CHURCH ST

STOP

PEARL ST

Three things you will need

1. Map = Bible

2. Guide =

3. Compass =

And he is the head of the body, the church. He is the beginning, the firstborn from the dead, that in everything he might be preeminent.

COLOSSIANS 1:18

2

pre·em·i·nent [prē-'e-mə-nənt] adj.
Origin: 15th Century Middle English,
Late Latin praeēminent.

Unravel the Travel

Take about 5 minutes to discuss these
questions with your mom or dad.

TRAVEL ADVISORY

**Challenges ahead.
Consider your options:**

- Run away and hide
- Give up
- Prepare to win

1. What's the biggest challenge you
   are facing in your life right now?

2. On a scale of 1 to 10 (1 indicates you have no confidence and
   10 indicates you are super-confident), how convinced are
   you that you'll be able to overcome this challenge?

3. What do you think you need to do in order to overcome it?

4. How can Mom or Dad help you?

TRAVEL ADVISORY

Traps have been spotted along the trail. Follow your map closely and pay attention to your guide.

Types of Traps

1. Lying to _____
2. _____
3. _____
4. _____
5. _____

WHAT TO DO IF CAUGHT IN A TRAP

1. ASK THE NEAREST BEAR TO HELP YOU OUT. REMEMBER TO USE YOUR INSIDE VOICE.

2. SCREAM AS LOUDLY AS YOU CAN. SURE, THIS WILL ALERT THE WILD ANIMALS, BUT YOU MIGHT GET LUCKY AND ANOTHER HUMAN WILL HEAR YOU FIRST.

3. LIE DOWN, BE STILL, AND TAKE A NAP. WHAT'S THE WORST THAT COULD HAPPEN?

TO AVOID TRAPS YOU NEED TO MAKE _____ _____ BASED ON YOUR _____.

CHILDREN, OBEY YOUR PARENTS IN THE LORD, FOR THIS IS RIGHT. "HONOR YOUR FATHER AND MOTHER" (THIS IS THE FIRST COMMANDMENT WITH A PROMISE), "THAT IT MAY GO WELL WITH YOU AND THAT YOU MAY LIVE LONG IN THE LAND." (EPHESIANS 6:1-3)

THE TEACHING OF THE WISE IS A FOUNTAIN OF LIFE, THAT ONE MAY TURN AWAY FROM THE SNARES OF DEATH. (PROVERBS 13:14)

Unravel the Travel

Identify the guides in your life. In the spaces below, list the people that you most respect and whose influence you want to follow.

P2P

PASSPORT2PURITY®
EXCURSIONS

TOUR GUIDES:

_____

_____

_____

_____

_____

_____

Your ultimate authority =
_____ and _____ _____

Your word is a lamp
to my feet and a
light to my path.

PSALM 119:105

Project: Puzzled

What will you think of when you remember this project?
Write your thoughts under the picture.

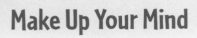

Make Up Your Mind

Take a few minutes to discuss what you've learned in this session with your mom or dad.

1. Why is it important for us to take extra time to talk about purity?

2. Are you nervous about some of the things we might talk about this weekend?

3. Explain to your parent what he or she can do to help ease your nervousness and to get the most out of your time together this weekend.

4. Remember the scripture that sets up our discussions about purity this weekend, Colossians 1:18: "And he is the head of the body, the church. He is the beginning, the firstborn from the dead, that in everything he might be preeminent." Why is it important to think of Christ when we talk about things like purity?

5. Since the Bible is our map, discuss some ways you can be more intentional about referencing the "map" in your day-to-day life.

VIRTUE, LIBERTY AND INDEPENDENC

PHIL

RUNNING WITH
2
THE HERD

Peer Pressure

peer ['pir] pres·sure ['pre-shər] noun, Origin: Middle English, from Old French per, equal, peer, from Latin pār; see pere-2 pressūra, from pressus, in Indo-European roots.

The power of a herd is an amazing thing. In nature, there are many good reasons for herds to gather: protection, identity, companionships. But the herd can also cause problems, leading many to follow in the wrong direction and destroying everything in its path.

WHOEVER WALKS WITH THE WISE BECOMES WISE, BUT THE COMPANION OF FOOLS WILL SUFFER HARM. PROVERBS 13:20

THE FEAR OF MAN LAYS A SNARE, BUT WHOEVER TRUSTS IN THE LORD IS SAFE. PROVERBS 29:25

Unravel the Travel

Who is in your herd? Identify the peers who have the most influence in your life by listing their names below.

⚠ TRAVEL ADVISORY

Running with a herd gives us a sense that we have value, that we are a part of something. But there are also challenges and risks involved.

Discuss your list with your mom or dad. If they don't know someone on your list, describe your relationship with that person.

TRAVEL ADVISORY
Conditions are favorable for peer pressure to occur.
Be aware of the following:

1. Everyone is susceptible to peer pressure.
2. Yes, even _____.
3. Your _____ will be tested.

Unravel the Travel

What would you do? Discuss Deb's Dilemma—the story you just listened to—with your mom or dad.

1. Do you think Deb handled this situation the right way?
Why, or why not?

2. What could she have done differently to handle it better?

3. What do you think you would do in a similar situation?

P2P Survival Manual

DON'T BE STAMPEDED BY PEER PRESSURE:
1. KNOW IN ADVANCE WHAT YOU WILL DO.
2. MAINTAIN THE COURAGE TO STAND FOR YOUR CONVICTIONS.

WHAT'S THE RISK OF GIVING IN TO PEER PRESSURE?
1. _____ _____ RUINS GOOD MORALS.
2. YOUR FRIENDS CAN HAVE A _____ INFLUENCE ON YOU.

> Do not be deceived: "Bad company ruins good morals." Wake up from your drunken stupor, as is right, and do not go on sinning.
>
> 1 CORINTHIANS 15:33–34

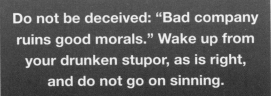

PPPO

PEER PRESSURE PROTECTION ORGANIZATION

FOR IMMEDIATE RELEASE

With the approach of peer pressure season, we wanted to remind you of proven ways that will help you avoid injury.

1. Be the influencer. Sure, your friends are affecting you, but you can affect them too.

2. Be on the alert for unusual behavior. If a friend acts one way when his or her parents are around and a different way when they're not, be cautious. A person of integrity and conviction is steady and reliable.

3. Being kind does not mean giving in. If you know you shouldn't join your friends in a certain activity, just say no. You don't have to be rude, but you should stand firm.

4. Asking for help is not immature. You're growing up and you're able to do more things on your own, but even adults need help. If you're concerned about some of your friendships, talk to your mom or dad about them.

5. Pray. You are never alone. God is listening.

Project: Mixing Friends

What will you think of when you remember this project?
Write your thoughts under the picture.

The people you spend time with will influence you. You will begin to be shaped and molded by them, whether the influence is good or bad. And bad company will corrupt. Your friends can cause your morals to decay if they do not share your convictions.

What do you look for in your friends?

A. What do you know about their _____? What are their desires? What are they most interested in?

B. What about their _____? Are their words clean and truthful? Do they talk about things they shouldn't? Do they tear down other people?

C. Where do their _____ look? What do they watch? What do they read? What kind of sites do they like to visit on the Internet?

D. Where do their _____ take them? Would you feel right about going to the same places they go? Would Christ approve?

Keep your **heart** with all vigilance, for from it flow the springs of life. Put away from you crooked **speech**, and put devious **talk** far from you. Let your **eyes** look directly forward, and your **gaze** be straight before you. Ponder [consider carefully] the path of your **feet**; then all your ways will be sure. Do not swerve to the right or to the left; turn your **foot** away from evil. (Proverbs 4:23–27, emphasis added)

LOOK CAREFULLY THEN HOW YOU WALK, NOT AS UNWISE BUT AS WISE, MAKING THE BEST USE OF THE TIME, BECAUSE THE DAYS ARE EVIL.

EPHESIANS 5:15–16

Unravel the Travel

Fill in the chart on the next page using the following instructions:

(1) Fill in the words that describe how you think an ideal friend would act in each of the categories listed down the first column.

(2) Write the names of your two or three closest friends in the empty boxes across the top of the chart.

(3) Referring back to the descriptions of heart, speech, eyes, and feet (from the previous page) do a quick checkup for each friendship you listed by

- placing a question mark (?) in any box where you have concerns about how that friend may be doing *(Remember: You are not trying to judge your friends, but are only trying to decide if you are choosing friends wisely.)* and

- placing a star (*) in any box where you feel that friend shows strong influence and whose example you feel you can follow without regret.

(4) Finally, what do you think your friends would say about you? In the last column, use the same (?) and (*) marks to indicate how you think you are doing in each of the same categories.

Before moving on, discuss your completed chart with your mom or dad.

Influence Chart

	heart	speech	eyes	feet
me				
ideal friend				

RUNNING WITH
2
THE HERD

You need to _____ :
_____
What you will do when pressured to do the wrong thing?

The Example of Daniel
(see Daniel 1)

Daniel determined in advance that he would stand on his convictions, even if it meant saying no to something that looked inviting. He showed respect to others without committing evil. He enjoyed God's favor and continued to trust and obey.

You need to know _____ you are and _____ you are here.

FOR WE ARE HIS WORKMANSHIP, CREATED IN CHRIST JESUS FOR GOOD WORKS, WHICH GOD PREPARED BEFOREHAND, THAT WE SHOULD WALK IN THEM.

EPHESIANS 2:10

> You are created in God's image.

> God has a mission for you—a unique purpose.

> Will you be a missionary or a _____ _____ ?

You need a personal relationship with Jesus Christ

As a young man I stepped into a lot of traps and disobeyed God, which is what the Bible calls _____. I was well aware that I had missed the mark and needed God's forgiveness for my sins.

> **Romans 6:23** For the wages of sin is death, but the free gift of God is eternal life in Christ Jesus our Lord.

"Death" means "_____ _____" from God. Because we've sinned against God we need God's forgiveness, we need a Savior.

> **Romans 5:8** But God shows his love for us in that while we were still sinners Christ died for us.

Jesus Christ did for you and me what we couldn't do for ourselves. He paid the penalty on the cross for our sins. But it's not enough just to know that He died for your sins. You need to personally place your faith in Him and give Him first place in everything.

> **John 1:12** To all who did receive him, who believed in his name, he gave the right to become children of God.

As a young man, I needed a personal relationship with Christ to help me resist temptations and avoid relationships that would negatively influence me. I realized if I was going to be the man God created me to be I needed to give Jesus Christ preeminence– _____ _____ in everything. It was at this point in my life that I asked Jesus Christ to be my Savior from my sins and to be the Lord, Master, and have first place in my life.

Make Up Your Mind
Part 1: Knowing God Personally

What about you?

Are things right between you and God? Is He the center of your life? Is His plan for your life your priority? Or is life spinning out of control as you seek to go your own way?

If you have been going your own way, you can decide today to ask Him to forgive all your sins and begin the process of changing you. You can turn to Christ, surrender your life to Him, and begin the adventure of allowing Jesus Christ and the Scriptures to transform your life. All you need to do is talk to Him in faith and tell Him what is stirring in your mind and heart.

Talk with your mom or dad about what you just read by discussing these questions together.

1. Do you have any questions about what it means to know God personally?

2. Have you received Christ as your Savior?

3. If you have, tell your mom or dad about it . . . When did it happen? How has your life changed as a result of that decision?

4. If you haven't, would you like to right now?

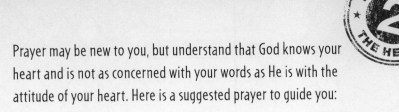

Prayer may be new to you, but understand that God knows your heart and is not as concerned with your words as He is with the attitude of your heart. Here is a suggested prayer to guide you:

> *Lord Jesus, I need You. Thank You for dying on the cross for my sins. I receive You as my Savior and Lord. Thank You for forgiving my sins and giving me eternal life. Make me the kind of person You want me to be. Amen.*

Make Up Your Mind (project optional)
Part 2: Peer Pressure

Discuss the following situation with your mom or dad.

You and three others are spending the night at your best friend's house. One friend opens his bag and pulls out a six-pack of beer that he smuggled in. Everyone begins drinking except you, and they begin to pressure you to do the same.

"One drink isn't going to hurt you," they say. "So what if your parents tell you that you can't drink alcohol? Do you think they always obeyed their parents? Do you think they never broke any rules?"

1. What would you do?

2. What are some things you think you'll be pressured by your friends to do in the next few years?

3. What do you think you need to do to resist negative peer pressure?

4. What can you do to have a positive influence on your friends?

PEOPLES REPUBLIC OF
CHINA
中国

J A P A N
NIPPON-KOKU
日本

BORDER CONTROL
26 -08- 2009
EXIT

READY FOR
3
AN UPGRADE?

NOTE: Young men, please turn to page 28.

for the young

women

TRAVEL ADVISORY
A. **Change is inevitable.**
B. **Your body is being bombarded by _____.**

- Breasts will grow rounder and larger.

- Hair will grow in new places (thicken on legs, under arms, on and around genitals).

- You will grow taller.

- Your pelvic bone structure and body fat will change.

- You will start your menstrual cycle.

- Body odor will increase.

- You may feel self-conscious or embarrassed about your appearance and the changes that are occurring.

- You may feel anxious about a lot of things that didn't bother you before (especially what other people think about you).

- You may find yourself more easily irritated or becoming angry over small things.

- You will have a growing desire for independence.

"Please, Aslan, . . . tell us when we can come back to Narnia again?" . . .

"Dearest," said Aslan very gently, "You and your brother will never come back to Narnia. . . . You are too old, children . . . and you must begin to come close to your own world now."[1]

---

[1] C.S. Lewis, *Voyage of the Dawn Treader* (New York: Scholastic, 1980), 247.

FOR YOU FORMED MY INWARD PARTS;
YOU KNITTED ME TOGETHER IN MY MOTHER'S WOMB.
I PRAISE YOU, FOR I AM
FEARFULLY AND WONDERFULLY MADE.
WONDERFUL ARE YOUR WORKS;
MY SOUL KNOWS IT VERY WELL.
MY FRAME WAS NOT HIDDEN FROM YOU,
WHEN I WAS BEING MADE IN SECRET,
INTRICATELY WOVEN IN THE DEPTHS OF THE EARTH.
YOUR EYES SAW MY UNFORMED SUBSTANCE;
IN YOUR BOOK WERE WRITTEN, EVERY ONE OF THEM,
THE DAYS THAT WERE FORMED FOR ME,
WHEN AS YET THERE WAS NONE OF THEM.

(PSALM 139:13–16)

You might be embarrassed by some of these changes. That is partly because young women tend to compare themselves to the other young women around them. Your friend's breasts may be developing faster than yours, or she may have started her menstrual cycle earlier than you, and you may feel inferior.

But you need to know, **and this is very important**, that it is not how quickly your body changes, or even the size of your breasts that matters, **but it is your heart for God and your desire to obey Him**. It is who you are in your _____ and the _____ _____ _____ that determine how quickly you grow to become a woman.

Resist the temptation to COMPARE.

Charm is deceitful, and beauty is vain, but a woman who fears the LORD is to be praised.

PROVERBS 31:30

Turn to page 32 for the remaining notes for this session.

for the young

men

TRAVEL ADVISORY
A. Change is inevitable.
B. Your body is being
   bombarded by _____.

- Your muscles will grow stronger.

- Your voice will begin deepening (and will take some time to even out).

- Hair will grow in new places (thicken on legs, under arms, on and around genitals, and possibly on chest and chin).

- You may feel self-conscious about your appearance and the changes that are occurring.

- Your penis will grow larger.

- You may feel anxious about a lot of things that didn't bother you before (especially what other people think about you).

- Body odor will increase.

- You may find yourself more easily irritated or becoming angry over small things.

- You will have a growing desire for independence.

"Please, Aslan, . . . tell us when we can come back to Narnia again?" . . .

"Dearest," said Aslan very gently, "You and your brother will never come back to Narnia. . . . You are too old, children . . . and you must begin to come close to your own world now."[2]

---

[2] C.S. Lewis, *Voyage of the Dawn Treader* (New York: Scholastic, 1980), 247.

FOR YOU FORMED MY INWARD PARTS;
YOU KNITTED ME TOGETHER IN MY MOTHER'S WOMB.
I PRAISE YOU, FOR I AM
FEARFULLY AND WONDERFULLY MADE.
WONDERFUL ARE YOUR WORKS;
MY SOUL KNOWS IT VERY WELL.
MY FRAME WAS NOT HIDDEN FROM YOU,
WHEN I WAS BEING MADE IN SECRET,
INTRICATELY WOVEN IN THE DEPTHS OF THE EARTH.
YOUR EYES SAW MY UNFORMED SUBSTANCE;
IN YOUR BOOK WERE WRITTEN, EVERY ONE OF THEM,
THE DAYS THAT WERE FORMED FOR ME,
WHEN AS YET THERE WAS NONE OF THEM.

(PSALM 139:13–16)

You might be embarrassed by some of these changes. That is partly because young men tend to compare themselves to other young men around them.

But you need to know, **and this is very important**, that it is not how quickly your body changes and how much hair grows on your chest or legs or face, or even the size of your penis that matters, **but it is your heart for God and your desire to obey Him**. It is who you are in your _____ and the _____ _____ _____ that determine how quickly you grow to become a man.

"As I look back over my life, I have to conclude that was the day I became a man. Turning twenty-one hadn't done it. A college degree hadn't done it. Even marriage hadn't made me a man. Nor having a son. Nor getting jump wings. Nor winning the Ranger tab. Nor wearing the Green Beret. But when I decided to follow Christ without reservation, I became a man. . . .

I believe it's impossible to be a man–fully masculine–apart from bowing to Jesus Christ as the Lord of your life and submitting to His Word as the ultimate life authority. A man's man is a godly man. A man's gotta do what a man's gotta do. And a man's got to make some decisions. Especially that one."

– Stu Weber, *Four Pillars of a Man's Heart*

> When I was a child, I spoke like a child,
> I thought like a child, I reasoned
> like a child. When I became a man,
> I gave up childish ways.
>
> 1 CORINTHIANS 13:11

What Is Sexual Intercourse?

Intercourse =

Sexual Intercourse =

Unravel the Travel

Take a few minutes to discuss these questions with your mom or dad.

1. Do you have any questions about anything you just heard?

Therefore a man shall leave his father and his mother and hold fast to his wife, and they shall become one flesh. And the man and his wife were both naked and were not ashamed.

(Genesis 2:24-25)

2. How do you feel about what you just heard?

3. Is there anything that did not make sense?

What the Bible Says about Sex

1. God designed it to be good.

2. Sex is for procreation.

   Procreation = "_____ _____."

3. Sex is for pleasure and closeness with your spouse.

   A person who has never had sex with another person is a _____.

4. God designed sex to bring Him glory.

   Your sexual conduct will communicate what you _____ about _____ and His purposes and His ways to the world. You will either say, "I believe His ways are right and good and I will follow them," or "I believe my way is the better way."

TODAY'S SPECIAL:

Sex _____

Comes with:

Side of
chili-cheese fries

Two double
cheeseburgers

An extra-large Coke

Top it all off
with a complimentary
gallon of ice cream

(Yes, you will be hungry!)

*"I adjure you,
O daughters of Jerusalem,
that you not stir up or
awaken love until it pleases."*

(SONG OF SOLOMON 8:4)

Project: Burned Up

What will you think of when you remember this project?
Write your thoughts under the picture.

Make Up Your Mind
Sexual Maturity Questionnaire

Take a few minutes to work on this part on your own.

1. What is your biggest question or fear about your body and how you are developing?

2. How do you think other preteens/teens view your physical and emotional maturity?

3. Before today, where have you been learning about sex? Place a checkmark next to the three or four that have influenced your thinking the most.

_____ Dad

_____ Mom

_____ Brothers/Sisters

_____ School

_____ Friends

_____ Church

_____ Media (TV, Internet, magazines, etc.)

_____ Other

4. What would you say is the purpose of sex?

5. What did you learn today about what the Bible says about sex?

6. With whom would you prefer to talk about sex?

Now, discuss your answers with your mom or dad.

**Purity means more than just not having sex.
Purity begins in your _____ and _____.**

Name _____

Address _____ Date _____

Watch over your heart with all diligence,
for from it flow the springs of life.
(Proverbs 4:23 NASB).

"For out of the abundance of the heart
the mouth speaks." (Matthew 12:34).

MD _____
Signature _____

The things that fill up your heart will
eventually spill out, so you want to be
careful to pursue purity in all the
things that influence your heart.

TRAVEL ADVISORY

Stay alert! Roadways often bordered by steep cliffs.

Boundaries:
Why should you set them?

- To protect yourself.

- If you don't set boundaries, someone else will set them for you.

How far will you go? . . .

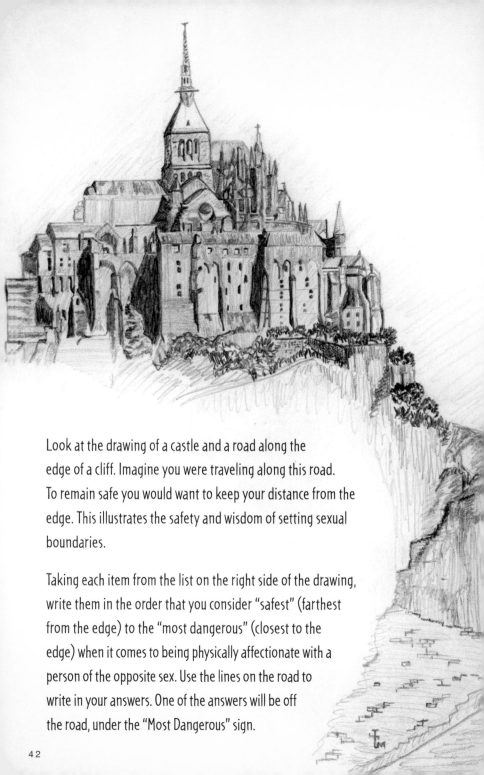

Look at the drawing of a castle and a road along the edge of a cliff. Imagine you were traveling along this road. To remain safe you would want to keep your distance from the edge. This illustrates the safety and wisdom of setting sexual boundaries.

Taking each item from the list on the right side of the drawing, write them in the order that you consider "safest" (farthest from the edge) to the "most dangerous" (closest to the edge) when it comes to being physically affectionate with a person of the opposite sex. Use the lines on the road to write in your answers. One of the answers will be off the road, under the "Most Dangerous" sign.

- Lying down while passionately hugging and kissing

- Kissing

- Touching below the neck

- Holding hands

- Touching below the waist

- Being alone with him or her

- Passionate hugging and kissing

- Sexual intercourse

- Hugging

- Taking clothes off

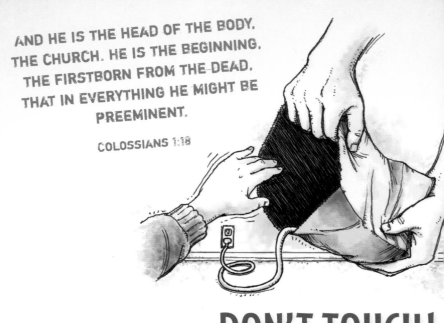

AND HE IS THE HEAD OF THE BODY, THE CHURCH. HE IS THE BEGINNING, THE FIRSTBORN FROM THE DEAD, THAT IN EVERYTHING HE MIGHT BE PREEMINENT.

COLOSSIANS 1:18

DON'T TOUCH!

Flee youthful passions.

2 TIMOTHY 2:22

Flee from sexual immorality.

1 CORINTHIANS 6:18

Abstain from sexual immorality.

1 THESSALONIANS 4:3

Where Does God Draw the Line?

1. You need to _____ God and His Word.

2. God doesn't say no to sex. He says yes to sex according to His _____.

3. God wants you to be sexually pure when you enter into marriage.

spent last night and today in Pamplona. Got to see the running of the bulls. No way! Scary, and I wasn't even in the street with the bulls. Made me think of Joseph. Running away doesn't always mean you're afraid. Sometimes it's the smartest thing to do.

Flee from sexual immorality. Every other sin a person commits is outside the body, but the sexually immoral person sins against his own body. Or do you not know that your body is a temple of the Holy Spirit within you, whom you have from God? You are not your own, for you were bought with a price. So glorify God in your body.

1 CORINTHIANS 6:18–20

How can you keep your way pure?

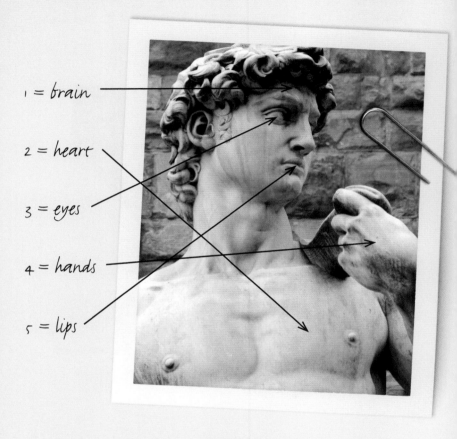

1 = brain

2 = heart

3 = eyes

4 = hands

5 = lips

1. _____ the right things. (Colossians 3:2)

2. _____ your heart. (Proverbs 4:23, Psalm 119:9–11)

3. _____ at the right things. (Psalm 101:3)

4. Keep your hands out of _____.

5. Keep your _____ off the opposite sex.

Project: Leaky Balloon

What will you think of when you remember this project? Write your thoughts under the picture.

For the Young Women

Men are stimulated by sight, touch, and attention.

Dress modestly

Watch the hugs

Don't flirt

Remember:
I'm trying to honor God, not attract boys

For the Young Men

As girls become young ladies, their bodies change. This can be an awkward time for them. Be respectful.

Don't tease

Treat girls with respect

Be a gentleman

Be honorable

Make Up Your Mind
Pursuing Purity

Discuss the following situation with your mom or dad.

You are at a party, and after a while you notice that several of your friends are pairing up with someone of the opposite sex. They find isolated corners around the house and begin to kiss and make out. You've been dancing with someone you've dated a couple of times, and they ask if you want to find a place to be alone together.

1. What would you do?

2. Why do you think God wants us to wait until marriage to be physically intimate with someone?

CROSSING
5
THE DATE LINE

Dating Questionnaire

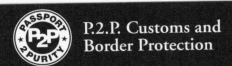

P.2.P. Customs and Border Protection

Application for Entry into the Country of: Dating

FORM APPROVED
OMB NO. 161-000

19 CFR 122.27, 148.12, 148.13, 148.110, 148.111, 1496, 31 CFR 5398

Instructions: Please accurately answer the following questions and submit this form for processing.

Name: _____ **Age:** _____

Current country of residence:

☐ Infancy ☐ Childhood ☐ Preteenager ☐ Teenager

Will you be bringing more than $10,000 cash into this country? ☐ Yes ☐ No

If so, please state on the back of this form where and how you acquired this much money.

Are you carrying any of the following items on your person?

Diamonds:	☐ Yes	☐ No
Exotic fruits:	☐ Yes	☐ No
Immature attitudes:	☐ Yes	☐ No
Farm soils:	☐ Yes	☐ No
Really bad breath:	☐ Yes	☐ No
Wood-eating insects:	☐ Yes	☐ No
Annoying behaviors:	☐ Yes	☐ No

(Please be aware that annoying behavior has been banned in our country since 2008.)

If you have any of the above items, please hand them over to a friendly customs agent before entering the country.

54

19 CFR 122.27, 148.12, 148.13, 148.110, 148.111, 1496, 31 CFR 5398

Please carefully answer the following questions to make clear your travel intentions while visiting our country:

What is dating?

What is the purpose of dating?

How old should you be to go on your first date?

What kind of person should you date?

Awkwardness Reduction Act Statement: This request is in accordance with the Awkwardness Reduction Act. Though it can be very awkward to submit this information, we ask for the information in order to carry out the regulations administered by the Customs and Border Protection. The form is used by Parents to apply for a duty allowance due to damaged or defective dating relationships and by CBP to authorize such an allowance. The estimated average awkwardness burden associated with this collection of information is 8 minutes per respondent depending on individual circumstances. Comments concerning the accuracy of this burden estimate and suggestions for reducing this burden should be directed to the Office of Dating and Budget, Awkwardness Reduction Project (1651-0007), Little Rock, AR 72223.

The Freedom from Awkwardness Act (FFAA), found in Title 5 of the Federal Republic of Dating Code, section 552, was enacted in 1973 and provides that any person has the right to avoid awkwardness in dating relationships. All agencies of the FRD government are required to disclose records upon receiving a written request for them, except for those records that are protected from disclosure by the nine exemptions and three exclusions of the FFAA. This right of access is enforceable in court. The federal FFAA does not, however, provide access to records held in places that we do not know about (since we don't know about them, that makes it difficult for us to access them now doesn't it?). Parents have their own statutes governing public access to unknown records; they should be consulted for further information about them.

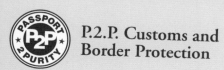

P.2.P. Customs and Border Protection

FORM APPROVED
OMB NO. 161-000

OFFICE OF THE FEDERAL REPUBLIC OF DATING

DIRECTOR OF ADMISSIONS: IMA N. AHUREE

Dear Sir/Madam:

This is your official notice that we have received your application for entry into our country. Upon initial review we realized that some of the answers on your customs declaration form were insufficient. Our office has thus been authorized to inform you more fully of the government policies for traveling in our country. Our travel consultants for incoming foreigners, Dennis and Barbara Rainey, will be in contact with you this weekend to provide further clarification and instruction. Please be prepared to capture the information they provide as answers to the following questions. You will need accurate answers to these questions to gain final approval for entry into our country:

1. What is dating?

2. What is the purpose of dating?

3. How old should you be to go on your first date?

4. What kind of person should you date?

Upon completion of this form, please submit three copies to the proper authorities for further review.

Ima N. Ahuree
Director of Admissions

Ima N. Ahuree

RECEIVED BY: *INA*

expedite

P.S. Please accept our sincerest apologies for the delay in processing your application. We eagerly await your clarification to the above questions.

Seeing Dating Differently

Your first step after receiving your stamped approval letter will be a tour of Dating City. Please make notes about each stop, because you will receive important information that you will need during your stay.

1 Focus on _____.

2 _____ to have a boyfriend or girlfriend.

3 Spend time in _____ _____.

4 REMEMBER: You are most likely spending time with _____ _____ _____ _____.

5 Don't _____ _____.

6 Don't act like _____ _____.

7 Off limits = _____ _____

Calle L.C. Ron

Hatibonico

Av. Camaguey

La Zambran

Av. Agra

3A 4A 5A

Cornelio Porro

alle Braulio Peñ

M. Suárez N.

4A

stopped to see a street performer play this song...

Philippians 2:3–5,8: Do nothing from rivalry or conceit, but in humility count others more significant than yourselves. Let each of you look not only to his own interests, but also to the interests of others. Have this mind among yourselves, which is yours in Christ Jesus.... And being found in human form, he humbled himself by becoming obedient to the point of death, even death on a cross.

Your Parents Need to Be Involved in Your Dating Experience

Your parents need to help you determine the following:

		GATE	
			17

Departure date: _____ you are mature enough to date

Travel companions: _____ you date

Checking in: _____ _____ about your relationships

Safety procedures: Set _____ and _____ your heart

BOARDING PASS

GATE 17

GATE CLOSES 1030

SEAT 23D

PASSENGER TICKET AND BOARDING PASS

This was an amazing trip. Found this magazine clipping with some questions to help me wrap it all up.

1. What boundaries are *you* going to establish to guard the purity of *your* heart?

2. Are you willing to wait to have a girlfriend or boyfriend?

3. Will you agree to what your parents say about dating?

Project: Too Close for Too Long

What will you think of when you remember this project?
Write your thoughts under the picture.

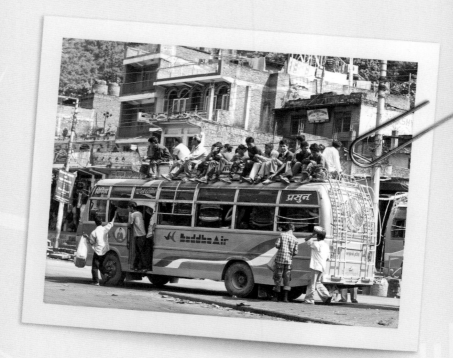

Make Up Your Mind

Answer the following questions on your own, and then discuss your answers with your mom or dad.

1. What boundaries are you going to establish to guard the purity of your heart? Be specific.

2. Are you willing to wait to have a boyfriend or girlfriend (that is, exclusive dating)?

3. Will you agree to what your parents say about dating: when to begin, whom you date, and how you ought to conduct yourself?

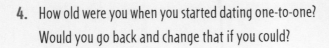

After discussing your answers with your mom or dad,
ask him or her the following questions:

4. How old were you when you started dating one-to-one?
    Would you go back and change that if you could?

5. Describe some of your own experiences in relating to the opposite
    sex. What was your experience in junior high, high school, college,
    after college, etc.?

6. What do you wish you would have done differently when it comes
    to dating?

7. What one key lesson would you pass on to me about dating?

Wait-to-Date Contract

To my parents,

Recognizing:

That God holds you accountable to raise me
in the admonition of the Lord,

That I am under your authority
as a child in this home, and

That you love me unconditionally and
are committed to my well-being,

I agree to wait until you believe I am
mature enough to go on a date.

_____

(Your signature)

_____

(Date)

_____

(Parent's signature)

AIR MAIL

R AVION

3 66

the journey Continues ➤

25 One-a-Day Devotions to Keep Your Heart and Mind Pursuing Purity

Space is left at the bottom of each daily reading for you to record your thoughts and responses. Some of the readings provide questions for further thought.

DAY ONE

Big Plans

Have you ever heard of Embu, Kenya? (Hint: It's in Africa.)

Emily Blake has.

She was twelve when she did something pretty extraordinary. She had heard that nearly ten million children under the age of five die every year from mostly preventable illnesses.[1] So she decided to help. Emily, who lives in Atlanta, Georgia, organized bake sales, car washes, a bowl-a-thon, and a concert. She sent out letters to family and friends.

At a youth retreat, Emily had taken in some powerful words from Pastor Louis Giglio. He "'challenged us to be more than just good kids,' Emily says. 'He challenged us to be kids so filled with love for our heavenly Father that we step out of our comfort zones and do great things for God.'"[2] Want to know what Emily's bake sales, car washes, and other work did?

It raised $40,000—enough money to start a Child Survival Program with Compassion International in Embu, Kenya. Then Emily went to visit Kenya, her bags stuffed with toys, bottles, and clothes for the mothers and babies she'd raised money for—babies who, with her help, would now survive.

In thinking about purity, sometimes it's easy to get caught up in all the things we shouldn't do. Watching everyone else, you might start feeling like you're the only kid sitting outside of an amusement park.

The reality? When you're choosing purity, you're choosing the adventure of a lifetime. You're saying no to things that poison and hurt, so you can say yes to something better than you can imagine. Purity is not just turning your attention away from things that hurt deeply; purity means being of only one substance (think of pure gold). It's about being totally devoted to God in everything. And that substance is a heart totally committed to God and the incredible dreams He has for your life.

Jesus said, "I came that they may have life and have it abundantly" (John 10:10). Get this: You're not missing out. He is the Creator of the universe, and He knows how life works best. He knows what hurts and what will pull you away from the "good works, which God prepared beforehand" (Ephesians 2:10).

God has shown He had incredible plans for Emily Blake. She's more than just a good kid. She lives out 2 Timothy 2:22, "So flee youthful passions and pursue righteousness, faith, love, and peace, along with those who call on the Lord from a pure heart."

What plans does He have for *you?*

So flee youthful passions and pursue righteousness, faith, love, and peace, along with those who call on the Lord from a pure heart. —2 Timothy 2:22

In what ways do you see that God's plan for your life is so much better than choosing a different path that leads away from purity? What needs do you see in the world that you would really like to do something about?

Creator God, thank You for loving me enough to have big dreams for me. Daily, give me the power to flee temptations so I can pursue You and Your kingdom. Help me to be more than just a good kid; I want to do great things for You.

---

[1] UNICEF, http://www.unicef.org/media/media_45485.html.

[2] Leanna Summers, "To Africa with Open Arms," *Compassion Magazine,* Fall 2009, 11.

Brain Science

Today, we're going to take a look at your brain. Everyone's got one. It makes you smile, helps you remember the capital of New Hampshire, makes your pancreas work, and helps you get a job. It pretty much does it all! So let's chat about your amazing brain—and the way yours is astoundingly different from someone's of the opposite sex.

You've probably heard of the hormone *testosterone*. The bodies of both males and females produce it, but men's bodies make about ten times more. Testosterone is powerful stuff. It makes muscles and bones grow larger, promotes aggressive behavior, and causes body hair.[1] It also increases sexual desire.

If testosterone were a caffeinated beverage, a nine-year-old boy would drink about a cup a day. But a fifteen-year-old boy would drink nearly two gallons a day—about twenty to twenty-five times more than what they were getting before adolescence. Not only that, but the area of a guy's brain that causes sexual pursuit is two and a half times larger than a girl's.[2] Getting the idea? From the way God made guys' brains alone, they naturally desire sex—and are on the lookout for it—a lot more than the average girl.

So here's the skinny: God is a big fan of sex. After all, He designed our brains and bodies for it. God knew that marriages would need the pleasures of a sexual relationship to bond a husband and wife together in unforgettable, complete, and intimate ways.

Yet we all know that in our culture, a guy can't get married easily at fifteen. (It'd be a bummer to be married and not be able to drive, for one thing.) So guys have these hormones that are priming their brains for connecting sexually with their wives . . . but it's not yet time.

Guys have an uphill battle for purity. God created most guys' brains to respond sexually through what they see. But in our world, guys never know when they're going to need to "bounce" their eyes off a raunchy billboard, a TV commercial with girls who aren't wearing much, or an underwear ad in Sunday's newspaper.

Guys, your eyes are your *responsibility*. Jesus made a direct tie between lustful glances and sins carried out in our hearts, saying that, "Everyone who looks at a woman with lustful intent has already committed adultery with her in his heart" (Matthew 5:28). It is not bad that you want to have sex, but be prepared to immediately make your sexual thoughts obedient to Christ (see 2 Corinthians 10:5).

Girls, you have an important responsibility to love your brothers in Christ well. Romans 14:13 reminds us, "Therefore let us not pass judgment on one another any longer, but rather decide never to put a stumbling block or hindrance in the way of a brother." What is one of the easiest ways to do this? Dress to honor God and the body He's given you, to treasure modesty. Clothes that are thin, tight, reveal a lot of skin, or don't cover your underclothes encourage guys to think about sex. *They can prompt guys to sin against God.* Though girls may want to feel sexually attractive, it would be wiser to care about the hearts of the guys around them.

All of us will abruptly find ourselves in contact with immodesty. Rather than judging people, we can pray for them. The more we understand how God has wired us, the more we can appreciate His creation and care for one another from the inside out.

> Women should adorn themselves in respectable apparel, with modesty and self-control —1 Timothy 2:9

---

[1] http://en.wikipedia.org/wiki/Testosterone.

[2] http://articles.cnn.com/2010-03-23/opinion/brizendine.male.brain_1_male-brain-mate-early-feminists?_s=PM:OPINION.

Bye-Bye, Baby

The eyes of the LORD are toward the righteous and his ears toward their cry. The LORD redeems the life of his servants; none of those who take refuge in him will be condemned. —Psalm 34:15, 22

You used to be a baby. It's hard to believe, but there was a time when you couldn't wipe your own nose, put on socks, roll over, make any intelligible noises, or even lift your head off the bed. You were completely and absolutely dependent on your parents for survival. From the moment you came out of the womb, if you had been left to fend for yourself, you would not have become the strong, smart, energetic young person you are today (making *mostly* intelligible noises).

So, thanks, Mom and Dad, for your utterly unrecognized labor of service. Thanks for changing all 2,190 of my diapers (yuck!), thanks for shoveling forty-seven pounds of pureed sweet potatoes into my mouth, thanks for turning your den into a staging area for the Salvation Army, and thanks for the courage to do these things instead of the many other things you could have been doing— other boring things such as hiking through Europe, serving on a remote mission field, learning to fly a helicopter, getting a master's degree in something that would make you more money, restoring a classic car, or pursuing a professional music career playing the glockenspiel.

Mom and Dad served you at a time when you needed it most. And they didn't do it begrudgingly (well, maybe sometimes, like at 3 a.m.). Nope, they wanted to serve you, wanted to make sure you stayed alive. In fact, those first few weeks they barely slept at night, acutely attuned to every whimper, whistle, and grunt that passed through your pipes. Their ears were active. And when you were on the floor during the day, their eyes were locked on you, watching every move you made, ensuring you didn't choke on a Lego or crawl into the fireplace.

God is like that with you as well. Psalm 34:15 says, "The eyes of the LORD are toward the righteous and his ears toward their cry." He cares deeply about you. He is interested in meeting your needs and protecting you from harm. And He's not just lounging around, waiting for you to come and beg for His help. No, He is active, on guard, constantly focused on your needs.

And here is the other exciting part: When you mess up, He's there to restore you. "The LORD redeems the life of his servants; none of those who take refuge in him will be condemned" (Psalm 34:22). Though He's watching, He's not standing over you ready to whack you when you mess up. He's there to restore you, set you back on your feet, and not condemn you.

So the next time you feel like complaining about not getting your favorite fruit snack for lunch, try to remember all those years that you don't remember, and just say "Thanks" instead. And also remember that God is personally interested in caring for you in many ways that you don't even realize.

Q: How does knowing that God is watching over you with such care make you feel?

Q: What are some things that God has protected you from over the last year?

DAY FOUR
Catherine of Aragon

The year 1488 is an interesting date in history. Young Catherine of Aragon, from Spain, married the British King Henry VII's son, Prince Arthur. Young indeed: Catherine was three, and Arthur was two. (Is it possible to get married before you're potty trained?)

This was a "marriage by proxy." People stood in the royals' places and recited their vows, and then Arthur and Catherine had a real wedding when he was finally old enough to marry. You know, when he reached fifteen.

Times have changed. Though toddler marriages may have been okey dokey in medieval England, they are less okay now.

Over and over in the Bible we're told there is a proper time for everything (check out Ecclesiastes 3:1-8 and Romans 5:6). There will be a proper time for you to look for a godly spouse to share your life with. For you, that's likely several years away.

Meanwhile, a part of us often still longs for a boyfriend or girlfriend. Most of us are honestly not ready to look for someone we'll be with forever. But nearly every person on the planet still wants to be loved intimately, completely, and unconditionally. We long for someone who thinks we're attractive, fills us with confidence, encourages us on bad days, hangs out with us, and does life with us. God made us that way–to long for relationships where we can be loved and where we can deeply love others.

When God had finished making Adam and the entire world, the Bible says over and over again that "God saw that it was good." There was no sin in the world, and Adam had God Himself as a companion. The only thing God saw that wasn't good? "It is not good that the man should be alone" (Genesis 2:18). God made us to be in relationships. Not only that, our relationships display God's love, "No one has ever seen God; if we love one another, God abides in us and his love is perfected in us" (1 John 4:12). We begin to understand how God loves us through the way other people love us.

Aha! Then I should go out and glorify God more and find myself a date!

Hold it! Here's where the "proper time" part comes in. Dating relationships almost always end in one of two ways:

1) You will break up.
2) You will get married.

Getting into relationships with the opposite sex before the right time can have a lot of regrettable consequences. In a way, dating is a little like Catherine and Arthur's toddler marriage; it's "practicing" until you're ready to get married. Unfortunately, you can get into a serious relationship before you have all you need to deal with it in healthy ways. These relationships can pull you toward sexual temptation and away from a lot of healthy things that make you a well-rounded person–activities and conversations with your friends, academics, and time with your family. It can even pull you away from being wholly devoted to God.

God has made a lot of great promises to those who wait on Him, who trust His perfect timing and plan for their lives. "Wait for the LORD; be strong, and let your heart take courage; wait for the LORD!"(Psalm 27:14). Rather than seeking a boyfriend or girlfriend, wait for God's timing, and spend your time seeking Him.

> I adjure you, O daughters of Jerusalem, that you not stir up or awaken love until it pleases.
> –Song of Solomon 8:4

DAY FIVE

Craving Dirt

True story: There are a handful of women who, when they're pregnant, crave dirt.

You've probably heard jokes about the foods pregnant women crave: pickles, ice cream, peanut butter and banana sandwiches. But dirt?

There's a disorder, *pica* ("pie-kah"), that people can get when their bodies lack vital minerals like iron. They need them so badly that things like sand and soil start to look yummy.

Mmm . . . dirt.

But pregnant women aren't the only people who crave. A philosopher, Blaise Pascal, observed, "There is a God-shaped vacuum in the heart of every man which cannot be filled by any created thing, but only by God, the Creator, made known through Jesus."[1]

Every single person you'll ever meet has one common craving. Whether they know it or not, they crave God.

It may not seem obvious. If people crave God, why are churches not stuffed with people? Why are Bibles not flying off the shelves like the latest novel?

Well, God created us with lots of desires to point us to *Him*, like hunger and thirst (He calls Himself the "Bread of Life" and "Living Water"). But even if we filled every other desire in our lives—the desire for friends, for family, the desire to feel liked and accepted, and every other desire—we would still find ourselves completely unsatisfied. Pascal had it right. We were made with a big, God-shaped vacuum inside of us that keeps pulling things in to try to fill it, like someone with pica eyeing a pile of dirt. If you don't start with God, nothing satisfies. *He* is what we need first and most. He made us that way.

God says in Isaiah 55:

Why do you spend your money for that which is not bread,
 and your labor for that which does not satisfy?
Listen diligently to me, and eat what is good,
 and delight yourselves in rich food.
Incline your ear, and come to me;

hear, that your soul may live. (verses 2–3, emphasis added)

When it comes to purity, this is important to understand. One of the reasons we're tempted toward impurity goes back to our not getting satisfied by God. Cravings push us into risking the *great* things God has for our future by compromising our purity now. We'd rather eat dirt than wait for the incredible meal God has for us in marriage. We don't really believe that He wants what's best—or that He'll sustain us while we wait for it.

Most times our cravings look like selfishness. We want what we want more than we love other people. Rather than caring for people, we might want to satisfy our desire to feel good or to relieve our fear of being alone.

When you're longing to be liked or loved, crossing the line of purity or giving in to peer pressure becomes a lot more tempting. You start to think your aching hunger could be filled, even just a little. You aren't trusting what God says—about how loved you are, how perfectly accepted you are apart from anything you do (because of Jesus), how completely known you are—so you look to have your "craving" met outside of God-honoring relationships.

What do you crave?

Satisfaction in God takes time. You can't just go down to the Spiritual Gas Station and get your God-tank filled. But being with Him, getting to truly know Him, and most of all, believing what He says, can be some of the best purity protection.

> Do nothing from rivalry or conceit, but in humility count others more significant than yourselves. Let each of you look not only to his own interests, but also to the interests of others. –Philippians 2:3-4

---

[1] Blaise Pascal, French mathematician and physicist, 1623–1662.

DAY SIX

Desperate for Light

One cave, three teens, and six flashlights. Seems like good odds, right? When the first flashlight quit an hour after they stepped into the darkness, it was no big deal; there were still five more torches blazing. An hour later two of the teens dropped theirs in the cold creek that ran along the cave's floor. Down to one light each. Time to turn around. At this point they were reminded of this crazy rule about old batteries: they run out. Over the next hour one light faded, then another. The three were left with one light between them and thirty minutes to the exit—thirty minutes to sunlight and life.

The leader barked out instructions, "Stay close—hands on shoulders. Watch your toes! Low stalactite on the right. Step up. Bats overhead—crouch down." The two in the rear obeyed dutifully. They moved as swiftly as possible, knowing their lives depended on it. Just one month prior, two youths were hospitalized for hypothermia after losing their lights in the same cave.

It's no surprise that they followed the light and the leader so carefully. Who wouldn't? Can you imagine if the teen in the back, the one farthest from the light, tried to bark out orders and direct the group? He would likely be left behind.

Psalm 119:105 says, "Your word is a lamp to my feet and a light to my path." God's Word is like a flashlight in a cave. It is the one thing in this life that is dependable in the darkness. The light of God's Word will clearly illuminate your path, but the question becomes, how closely will you choose to depend on it? Will you completely trust your life to it? Or will you choose to go your own way? Ignoring the counsel of God's Word in this crazy, upside-down world is just as crazy as shutting off your one remaining light when you're thirty minutes from the mouth of the cave.

Proverbs 8:19-20 says, "My fruit [the benefits of following wisdom] is better than gold, even fine gold, and my yield than choice silver. I walk in the way of righteousness." Following God's Word as closely as you would a fading flashlight in a dark cave will bring greater reward in your life than huge piles of gold and silver. Walking this path is the one true way to really live.

After many stubbed toes and knocked noggins, the three friends rounded the final bend in the cave with only a flicker of light left. They made it. Once safely outside, they vowed never to return again. Well, at least not without more flashlights (preferably waterproof) and new batteries. And maybe even a few emergency glow sticks. Oh, and a few more snacks as well. I mean, who wants to be stuck in a cave without good snacks?

Q: What one sentence would you write to describe your level of dependence upon God's Word today?

Q: How can you increase your dependence upon God's Word? How can you come to follow it more?

Dirty Socks

Ever worn white socks outside without shoes? Did everything they touch become white?

Uh, doubt it. By the time you went back inside, the bottoms of your socks were probably a nice shade of grayish brown with little pieces of yuck stuck all over them. If you accidentally stepped in a muddy spot you can bet the person washing your laundry was less than tickled about it.

Choosing friends can be a little like wearing white socks.

The Bible has an interesting verse about this, "Do not be deceived: 'Bad company ruins good morals'" (1 Corinthians 15:33). You might come away from your Passport2Purity experience geared up about serving God with your whole heart and your whole body. But let's say in a couple of years—or days—you're hanging with friends who talk rudely about their parents. Let's say these same friends you go to sleepovers with, share sodas with, and play sports with start kissing their boyfriends or girlfriends and maybe going a little further. Maybe they are going to cool parties on weekends where there just happens to be some less-than-pure stuff going on.

Chances are, your own socks are going to start getting dirty.

Even if you are an incredibly strong person with a lot of maturity, a higher-than-average ability to say no, and a desire to share Jesus with your friends, we are all influenced by other people. You may not be the one making out at a party or holding a cup of beer, but you're naturally going to want to fit in somehow. Maybe it will be your language or a few unkind comments about other people. It could be even more subtle; you could start thinking less about how to honor God and more about the shady stuff your friends are talking about.

You get the idea: dirty socks. You can't walk around outside and expect your socks not to tell the tale. Really mixing it up with people and getting involved in their lives to show them Jesus is one thing; Jesus ate meals and had great conversations with people who weren't following God. But choosing *close* friends who don't know God is another. Jesus, in fact, chose men who loved God with their lives to be his three closest friends. The Bible says, "Do not be deceived." No matter how strong you are, *bad company ruins good morals.*

Let's say that you ask God to give you a solid friend, one who really loves Him and seeks Him out. Imagine that this friend God gives you to munch your lunch with, talk on the phone with, choose a movie with, and laugh with until milk comes out your nose is also spending time in God's Word. Let's imagine that you decide together to go to the youth retreat. You both say no to the marijuana joint or dirty magazine that someone is passing around. This friend's not perfect. But when you're having the worst day, you remind each other that God has a plan for you both. You pray for each other. Your lives are going in the same general direction: following Jesus.

It could be a big help in keeping your socks white.

Keep this in mind: *Your friends will help determine who you become.* Yes, be a bright light that shines Jesus like bleached-out socks to the world! But make sure that your closest friends are going in the same direction—not pulling you the opposite way. You don't need to be a Lone Ranger. Find someone else who also wants clean socks.

DAY EIGHT
Don't Mind if I Do

We've talked quite a bit about the importance of "making up your mind" in advance in order to be able to withstand peer pressure. But making up your mind is not always an easy thing to do. Herds of supercharged emotions and desires can barrel right through your brain, trampling over your willpower without looking back.

How do you stop the stampede in your brain and stand firm for the truth? Romans 8:13 says, "If by the Spirit you put to death the deeds of the body, you will live." How do you "put to death" a sin before it even gets started? By attacking it in your mind. Kris Lundgaard, in his book *The Enemy Within*,[1] offers the following encouragement for battling sin in your mind:

1) ***Think about the sovereignty of God.*** Think about the great Lawgiver who forbids sin. Think, *It is God who forbids this; the great Lawgiver, who rules in sovereignty over me, on whom I depend for every breath of life, and from whom I can expect my lot in this life and the next* (see how Joseph did this in Genesis 39:9).

2) ***Think about the punishment of sin.*** Keep in mind that "our God is a consuming fire" (Hebrews 12:29). To forget this or ignore this is to slap God in the face (Romans 1:32). Jesus counseled us to fear Him "who can destroy both soul and body in hell" (Matthew 10:28).

3) ***Think about all the love and kindness of God, against whom every sin is committed.*** When God's love touches your soul and moves you, and you know that every sin is against the Lover of your soul, you are less likely to give in to sin.

> "Do you thus repay the LORD,
>   you foolish and senseless people?
> Is not he your father, who created you,
>   who made you and established you?" (Deuteronomy 32:6)

4) *Think about the blood and mediation of Christ.*
"For the love of Christ controls us . . . and he died for all, that those who live might no longer live for themselves but for him who for their sake died and was raised" (2 Corinthians 5:14-15).

5) *Think about the indwelling of the Holy Spirit.* If you fully consider how sin grieves the Spirit, how it defiles His dwelling place, how you lose and forfeit His comforts by it–this works against the lusting of sin.

Take some time right now to identify one particular sin that has been an ongoing struggle for you. Which of the five ideas above will best help you fight this sin in your mind?

Spend some time praying for the Spirit to help you gain ground over this sin. Try writing out your prayer below.

Finally, try memorizing one of the above scriptures and calling upon it when you're fighting that sin.

---

[1] Adapted from Kris Lundgaard, *The Enemy Within* (Phillipsburg, NJ: P&R Publishing, 1998), 85–88.

DAY NINE
Don't Drink the Water

Fact: There are countries around the world where you definitely should *not* drink the water.

It's pretty nice that most of us reading this can walk over to a sink and get a drink. Our bodies are 73 percent water. Pure water equals not only our ability to survive but to thrive–to live life to its potential.

Yet a large number of people don't have that privilege. In a glass, their water might look okay. But if you take a little sip, you may regret it. There are all sorts of organisms that your digestive system will revolt against. *MUST... GET... THEM... OUT!* You could get very sick, even for months. Don't brush your teeth in it, wash dishes in it, or open your mouth in the shower. It equals bad news.

That water is undrinkable because of its contaminated source. Whether underground or from a lake or reservoir, it's a place where billions of itty-bitty creatures are having all sorts of fun making more of themselves. What gushes out of the faucet may look harmless, but the water is bad because its source is bad.

And here's the reality about your life: Purity, resisting peer pressure, and making right choices are wonderful things to do–truly great goals. If you have committed yourself to purity, way to go! Kudos to you for a wise and courageous decision.

But just encouraging you to live purely would be leaving you with just a bunch of good advice unless you learn the whole truth: Unless your *heart* is made pure by God, your actions can't be truly pure and life-giving. It's God changing us on the inside that makes the adventure of a pure life possible.

Even if you attempted to make all the right decisions, if you're not clean inside, your actions are contaminated. The "water" coming out of your heart may look okay. But the Bible says unless we do right actions from a heart that loves and worships God, it's like painting a grave white: It's still full of dead men's bones. Your "water" is contaminated. A pure life comes from a pure heart.

Each of us has done wrong things. We hurt people. We lie. We think terrible thoughts. We're selfish and self-centered. The Bible calls it *sin*.

Yet despite the people we all truly are inside, God loves us enough to pay the penalty for our sin (death!) Himself. He became a person, Jesus, who lived a life uncontaminated by sin. Then He died a brutal death here on earth, pouring out His blood so we could be forgiven and have a relationship with Him. We can become pure like Him, living out all the great things He intended. Jesus even conquered death by rising from the dead. He demonstrated that we, too, can have new life after the death of sin.

When you accept His payment and forgiveness, the Bible says you're a new creation: The old contaminated you has gone; inside, the new has come. Your pure life starts *there*. His Holy Spirit begins to retrain your heart and behavior. His power fuels you to choose a conquering life uncontaminated by sin—and leads you again to God's forgiveness when you don't.

As you go out to make real choices in real life, remember that a pure life *only* flows out of a pure source.

"Either make the tree good and its fruit good, or make the tree bad and its fruit bad, for the tree is known by its fruit." –Matthew 12:33

You and three of your best friends are hanging out, maybe around the pool, practicing flips and dives and consuming more water than watermelon. The summer sun is shining, a light breeze moves across droplets of sweat running down your glass of ice water, and as you look across the pool to watch a friend turn another backflip into a belly flop, you see a dozen men, large men in uniforms with guns, big guns, walking toward you. They tie up your arms, drag you into a waiting truck, and haul you and your friends away. Soon you are on an airplane heading across the ocean to another country. You don't know it at the time, but you will never again see your home or your family.

It's hard to imagine something so crazy happening, but in the history of the world it has been more common than you'd think. Raiding armies would pillage other lands and kidnap their best and brightest youth (yes, just like you and your friends). They would then turn these young, impressionable, talented people into slaves. Some were lucky and were put to work in the palace assisting the king; but others were sent to do the dirty jobs like cleaning the toilets, which were not like our indoor porcelain pots with running water.

This happened in the Old Testament, when Daniel and his best buds were whisked away to Babylon. The first thing their new king did was change their names. Their birth names were connected to the God of Israel (Daniel, "God has judged," and Azariah, "The LORD helps," for example). But their new names were tied to the Babylonian gods like Baal and Nebo—not a great start. But the changes didn't stop with their names; food, language, writing, books—all were changed. In fact, from the moment these young men arrived, every action was meant to change their allegiances, identity, and values from Jewish to Babylonian.

How did Daniel react to all of this being forced upon him? The Bible says, "Daniel made up his mind that he would not defile himself with the king's choice food or with the wine which he drank" (Daniel 1:8 NASB). Daniel would not cast aside what he had learned from childhood without a fight. He was willing to risk losing a premium place in the palace to stand for what he knew was right.

Now, it may be hard to put yourself in Daniel's sandals, but think about yourself: What beliefs are you tempted to give up because of recent changes in your life? You probably did not move to Babylon this year, but maybe a new school or neighborhood or church? Is there something right now that you are being asked to forsake by a new friend, something important?

Q. What can you do to help "make up your mind," as Daniel did, to stand for your convictions before you lose sight of what you know to be true?

DAY ELEVEN
Enticed

My son, if sinners entice you, do not consent. –Proverbs 1:10

He had a choice to make. The gun was pointed at his head. Would he give in, or would he stand for what was right? He had only a few seconds to make up his mind. Agree to go along, and the gun lowers–life goes on. Refuse, and the trigger is yanked back sending a small, round, shiny object to bounce off his skull. No doubt it would hurt and leave a nasty mark, but being shot by a BB pistol isn't the end of the world.

They had sneaked out of his friend's house late at night to run around the neighborhood. Harmless fun, right? But what he didn't know was that his friend had a different plan: Sneak over to a loathed neighbor's house and shoot out a window with a BB gun. So there they stood, just steps from the window with the friend ready to pull the trigger. But when the friend was called out for his juvenile sense of justice, he went defensive, demanding compliance.

Proverbs 1:10 opens with the personal address, "My son." King Solomon, the wise king, was writing down some of his best sayings, wisdom for life, for his son. And one of the first things he says is, "If sinners entice you, do not consent." In fact, he spends the next nine verses giving further explanation to the ways sinners would try to entice his son (Proverbs 1:11-19). Why avoid the enticement of sinners? Solomon explains in the next chapter, "Discretion will guard you, understanding will watch over you, *to deliver you from the way of evil"* (Proverbs 2:11-12 NASB, emphasis added).

Solomon's desire was to protect his son, and the wisdom of God's Word would provide such protection. When you walk with the wise, you will also be wise; but when you dance with delinquents, you might end up with a gun pointed at your head.

So what would you do in this situation? Walk away and face a sting to the backside, or worse, a shot that puts your eye out? Sure, it will hurt, but is it life threatening? Is it worth the compromise? Of course, you aren't pulling the trigger, so why not go along with it?

What would you do?

Read through the rest of Solomon's charge to his son to avoid sinners (Proverbs 1:11–19).

The ancient Greek philosopher Socrates wrote about how important it is to "know thyself," meaning to know what you are like, how you are wired, and how you think and act. One way to prepare for temptation is to know how you are most likely to be tempted–to know yourself.

Which of the temptations Solomon listed for his son are most likely to entice you? (Note: A good way to know where your weaknesses are is to think about where you have faced the most temptation in the past.)

Finally, is there someone you can admit this temptation to? Someone who can pray for you, maybe a parent or a friend? Write the person's name below, and plan a time to talk with them about it sometime this week.

DAY TWELVE
Eyes Above

Imagine you're getting ready to go backpacking. You're staying in the wilderness for a few days and bringing a friend. You can practically smell the pine-scented air and smoldering logs. There's nothing like the simplicity of having everything you need on your back.

Which is why you are surprised when your friend walks out of the house with his tuba. Oh, and his DVD player. And a coat stand. Huh? He goes back in: Can't forget the waffle iron.

Dude, you're thinking, *we've gotta carry everything on our backs. We're only staying three days. What's with the Christmas ornaments and the tennis racket?*

Backpacking is about temporary living. So why is he packing the snorkel and flippers? You can't carry the essentials–including food and toilet paper–if you're weighed down with all this stuff that keeps you from getting to the campsite in the first place and wouldn't help if you could. "Wouldn't help!" exclaims your friend. "Haven't you ever wondered where you could hang your coat in the wilderness? Hel-lo! Problem solved. Coat stand!"

The truth is, it's easy to do this in life. We've been on earth long enough that we start acting like this is where we'll be forever. We get so distracted by what is here that we stop "carrying" the things that last, the things we need, the things that really matter.

The Bible commands us, "Set your minds on things that are above, not on things that are on earth" (Colossians 3:2). Or as Jesus put it:

> **"Do not lay up for yourselves treasures on earth, where moth and rust destroy and where thieves break in and steal, but lay up for yourselves treasures in heaven . . . For where your treasure is, there your heart will be also"** (Matthew 6:19–21).

He's right. (No surprise there.) Everything on this planet has an expiration date whether it's a mullet, a VHS collection, an iPod, an athletic record, or a reign as homecoming queen. Are the things your mind is fixed on going to be important for as long as your soul lives–for eternity?

Most of the world around us–including music, movies, ads, and the stuff other kids see as important–is running after things for *right now*. You might be persuaded to just do what makes you feel good or look good. Having popularity, money, success, beauty, or whatever you want can all be good things. Proverbs tells us over and over to make wise decisions in how we work, speak, handle money, and relate to others; these things honor God and affect us for the long haul. (So your parents know what they're talking about when they press you to work hard at school, clean your room, and take a shower.) In fact, God is very clear that how we handle things here has effects in eternity.

But a lot of the things we run after can stand in His place. They can be what you "pack" in your life's backpack of essentials. We act like these things are our food, sleeping bag, or flashlight, when really we're bringing the equivalent of coat hangers and a mop. Good things, but they're taking the place of what really matters.

So it's critical to ask and answer honestly, over and over: What are my treasures? What do I want? What will I give my life to?

As you prepare for a quiz, practice for the game, or decide what to do with your spare time, ask: What will it look like, in every activity and thought, for my mind to be on things above?

Fade Away

A basketball autographed by Michael Jordan himself!

Steven Helmick could hardly believe it was his—completely, permanently his. Steven, a point guard for his junior high school team, had been playing basketball since first grade. And this year the gym seriously needed a new air conditioner. So the team members created a competition and found sponsors who would pay them for each free throw they could make in ten minutes time.

Steven had made 120 free throws. He could still recall the crowd's cheer, the ache of his biceps after ten straight minutes of shooting, the disbelief that he'd won the competition—and the ball. The basketball autographed by Air Jordan was now his for the rest of his life. Who knew how much it would be worth in ten, twenty, even fifty years?

Steven was determined to protect his new treasure. He bought a clear acrylic display cube and placed the ball inside, resting it on his dresser for daily inspiration.

What did Steven not anticipate? The light that poured through his bedroom window right through the plastic cube eventually faded the signature beyond recognition. He had underestimated one of the forces that seeped right into his own bedroom, robbing the basketball of its worth.

Your sexual purity can be a little like that basketball. As you collide with different temptations, friends, and situations, you might be persuaded to redefine purity. *If I do this, it's not technically crossing the line.* Or even, *If I do this, it doesn't count as sex.* Or, *Well at least we didn't do that; I still have my purity.*

Actions like these are like a display cube: helpful for keeping out some destruction, sure, but they can't block out the inerasable, intended-for-marriage effects of sex that leave our purity almost unrecognizable.

Purity is not just a trophy to remind you of something accomplished; it has lasting value. It has meaningful and *lasting* effects on your life.

Purity, by definition, is freedom from any substance that spoils. The focus of our sexual purity isn't what we *don't* do. It's not about seeing how much we can do and still be considered pure. It's a spotlessness of heart: a heart totally dedicated to God, faithful to your future spouse and marriage, and committed to the perfect way God designed relationships to work. It's that singularity of substance that results in decisions that keep our bodies pure. It's not asking how little we can give God and our future spouse; it's asking how much we can give them.

Protect the treasure of sexual purity God has given you—and not just from the act of sex. Use the Bible's standard:

> But among you there must not be even a hint of sexual immorality, or of any kind of impurity . . . because these are improper for God's holy people. –Ephesians 5:3 NIV

DAY FOURTEEN
Fast Food

Morgan Spurlock, documentary filmmaker, had an interesting idea for a movie (*Super Size Me*): Go to three doctors for full checkups, then eat nothing but fast food from one restaurant chain for a month–breakfast, lunch, and McDinner. Super-size your meal when asked. Don't exercise. At the end, get more physicals, and find out what happened.

At his first round of checkups, Morgan was in great health. He was about 6'2", 185 pounds, and his body fat levels were well below average at 11 percent.

Want to know what happened?

Morgan gained twenty-five pounds–ten of those in one week. His body fat rose to 18 percent. His liver showed signs of disease, like someone who had been doing some serious drinking. Emotionally, he felt depressed after he ate the restaurant's food. It took Morgan eight weeks to recover a healthy liver and over a year to lose the weight.

Ugh.

Compare this experience to what Spurlock found when he visited an alternative school in Appleton, Wisconsin–alternative because it's for kids with such behavior problems that they have a hard time making it in regular schools. The school naturally had a lot of issues such as drugs and enough violence to require the presence of police. That's when the school overhauled its lunch menus: the pizza and corn dogs kind were replaced with fruits, veggies, whole grains, and lean meat.

Want to know what happened?

Grades and concentration levels went up. The number of kids missing class, being expelled, fighting, and dropping out went way down. The faculty was amazed at the diet's effect on academic performance and behavior.

Now, before you wonder if purity somehow depends on veggies, don't worry. You can still have a Big Mac. But pay close attention. Morgan Spurlock proved in a very real way that we are what we eat.

And there's another way we become what we take in: what we feed our minds.

There are lots of verses that tell us what the diet and exercise of our minds should look like. Try Philippians 4:8:

> **Whatever is true, whatever is honorable, whatever is just, whatever is pure, whatever is lovely, whatever is commendable, if there is any excellence, if there is anything worthy of praise, think about these things.**

Romans 12:2 also encourages us, "Do not be *conformed* to this world, but be *transformed* by the renewal of your mind" (emphasis added).

Let's say we choose a diet of *brain* junk food–like TV shows that value completely different ideas of love and sex from those of the Bible. We snack on a little junk through the off-color lyrics in our music. We grab another helping of junk with a side of junk flipping through a magazine full of airbrushed ideas of beauty, immodest clothes, and kissing techniques. We super-size it with some lewd conversations at school. Our minds are feasting on the equivalent of nonstop fries and nuggets. It's fun and tasty, but it's starving us from what would really nourish and satisfy–as in the Bread of Life (see John 6:35). It poisons our thoughts; garbage in, garbage out. That brain junk food is taking us in the opposite direction of God's kingdom.

There are lots of moments ahead when you'll be tempted without warning to indulge in some brain candy. But remember, you are what you eat. Your ideas are sometimes altered in tremendous ways by what you choose to take in. And it could take years to get rid of that kind of poison.

Don't give in. Choose mind food that really satisfies.

> I will not set before my eyes anything that is worthless. I hate the work of those who fall away; it shall not cling to me. –Psalm 101:3

DAY FIFTEEN
Fear of Traps

Complete this statement: I'm very afraid of _____.

What was the first thing that came to mind? Snakes? Spiders? Tiny space aliens living in your closet? Maybe it was something a little more serious, like failing in school or losing a loved one or getting really sick.

A woman was listening to a radio program when she heard the teacher ask this very question. After thinking for a moment, she said to herself, "Losing all our money; that's what I'm most afraid of." The teacher, seemingly reading her thoughts, responded, "If you answered anything other than, 'Allowing my relationship with Christ to become less important in my life,' then your fears are out of balance." Ouch. That realization hit her hard. How had money become so important in her life? Didn't Jesus promise that God—who cares for the birds of the air who have no home—would meet our needs as well (Matthew 6:26-30)?

Proverbs 29:25 says, "The fear of man lays a snare, but whoever trusts in the LORD is safe."

Usually, "the fear of man" means being more worried about what people think of you than what God thinks of you. It means making decisions that please your friends or some other person first and foremost rather than God. Being more worried about what people think than what God thinks will "lay a snare" in your life. It will cause problems; it will hinder you, weigh you down, and keep you from following God's plan for your life.

This kind of thinking is a ruse that will snap shut on you like a hidden bear trap. It's as if you are hiking along in the Alaskan wilderness, and everything is amazing. The birds are chirping, and you're whistling a melody to match. The air is fresh; a cool stream flows by on your right, and with the next step, BLAM! Your leg is snapped in two. You just went from happy hiker to wolf bait—not good.

Proverbs 29:25 talks about the fear of man, but really, any fear "lays a snare" or sets a trap in your life. The beautiful part of this verse is the promise of safety found in trusting the Lord. Trusting Him is like following a guide on that Alaskan wilderness trail and watching him point out every trap along the way, protecting your leg from that feeling nobody wants.

Trusting the Lord will protect you from the dangerous snare set by your fears and will maybe even keep you from an unseen bear trap or two.

Q. Look back at the fear you identified at the beginning. Why do you fear that so much?

Q. How has this fear been a snare in your life?

Q. What can you do to help reduce this fear?

Look up a few of the following verses and write down one that is especially meaningful to you: Psalm 23:4; Psalm 27:1-3; Psalm 46:1-3; Psalm 66:16-20; Psalm 118:5-7; Isaiah 43:1-2; Luke 12:4-5; Romans 8:14-16; 2 Timothy 1:7.

DAY SIXTEEN
Fire Power

Imagine a world without fire.

Many of the world's cities would have remained intact, untouched by the fires that devastated landmarks and homes and took so many lives: Rome, Constantinople, Amsterdam, Moscow, London, Tokyo, Chicago, and Copenhagen. Every year the five million acres that are lost to wildfires would be saved. There would be no guns as we know them, which operate with a spark. In fact, there would be no explosions of any kind—even nuclear weapons. No fireworks injuries; no hospital burn units. That doesn't sound so bad!

But here's what we probably couldn't get over: Until the discovery of alternate heat sources like electricity, humanity would consume uncooked meat, unbaked bread, and everything else raw. No heated water, no lights in the dark, no heat for killing germs on food, dishes, and clothing. No cars, whose engines also function with a spark. We would have very few sources of warmth for most of human history and for the majority of the world right now. No sun, in fact! Without fire, humanity could not exist.

Fire is powerful. Clearly, when it's out of control fire can bring tragic, deadly consequences. But within boundaries, it's also done a great deal of life *saving* for all of humankind.

Sex can be powerful in a similar way. Here's the kicker: God is a big fan of sex—which He created. There is an entire book of the Bible dedicated to this marvelous part of creation. (Note: He used sex to make you.) This is not just because sex makes people in the form of cute little babies. God carefully and fabulously designed sex to glue married couples together in their bodies, minds, and hearts all at the same time in a private, exclusive way, over and over. They don't have to be ashamed when they are revealing all of themselves—when nothing is hidden. They can be completely truthful about themselves and still be completely loved.

From the beginning of the Bible, we see that one of God's deep loves is unity. He loves the oneness of Himself in three persons.[1] He makes great personal sacrifices to make us one with Him. He loves when, as His people, we are united together with Jesus as our Master.[2] God starts the Bible with a wedding–Adam and Eve's–and ends the Bible with a wedding–Jesus and His Bride, the Church.[3] God designed that a marriage, where two people become "one flesh," represent Him to the world.

And it works! The ways our bodies physically react to sex and the ways our hearts and minds respond to sex and remember it are powerful. Sex is God's idea, and it is breathtaking, amazing stuff . . . when used as directed.

Because sex, like fire, is so powerful, it can be equally destructive when it leaps out of its created boundaries. Yes, there are lifelong consequences like AIDS, STDs, and pregnancy. Even without those, there are consequences that are hard to see but just as real. They leave scars that can affect your relationship with your spouse for years–potentially jeopardizing an out-of-this-world, spectacular sex life. God created this unifying act to be beautifully repeated and developed over a lifetime, a secret kingdom.

God wrote the instruction manual for the firepower of sex. Use it wisely, and you'll be basking in its glow for a lifetime.

> Therefore a man shall leave his father and his mother and hold fast to his wife, and they shall become one flesh. And the man and his wife were both naked and were not ashamed.
>
> –Genesis 2:24-25

---

[1] See Deuteronomy 6:4 and Matthew 28:19.
[2] See John 17:11, 20 and Ephesians 4:1–6.
[3] See Genesis 2:18–25 and Revelation 21:1, 9.

DAY SEVENTEEN

Groupthink

Have you ever been in a situation where the right answer seems so obvious, but nobody's saying it?

Let's say you're with a group, sitting in a room with a poster of a huge triangle. Someone walks in and asks what shape is on the wall. Everyone but you says, "A square."

You're thinking, *Huh?*

You speak up. *This is so dumb.* "It's a triangle." *Hello!*

But everyone else keeps insisting it's a square. Straight lines, angles—this is a square. Pretty soon, even the person who asked the question is looking at you like you just stopped in on your way to Mars.

You're thinking, *No way. Are these people serious?* You keep looking around, trying to figure out what's going on, and wondering where in the world these people went to preschool.

Would you ever give in?

Strange, but true: Scientists have conducted experiments like this, secretly telling all but one person to insist on something that's obviously wrong. And believe it or not there are some people who have given in, agreeing with the rest of the group: *I must be wrong. I have no idea how, but I must be wrong.*

In real life, it happens even with adults. For years, scientists have been amazed by what they call "groupthink." People get into a group, and they can all start thinking the same thing even if it's dead wrong. Sometimes it's because someone doesn't speak up. Sometimes a leader makes fun of the person who disagrees with everyone else, making the person feel stupid. Governments have even made poor decisions based on groupthink.

You have probably even seen this happen when a bunch of friends get together. In fact, it could happen with your friends, and they might start going in a direction you know is wrong. The tough part is having the courage to say or do what you know is right—to be a "triangle" type of person.

It can be truly hard, because a lot of times what we want is more powerful to us than the desire to do what's right. Sometimes, to be seen as cool (or at least not seen as a nerd) or to stay comfortable and not be ridiculed by friends is way easier than saying, "Dude, that's a triangle–duh," or "That's wrong."

The good news? You are never alone. You know it's true; God is with you. Not only that, but if you've trusted Jesus as your Savior and Master, His Holy Spirit is in you. He gives you not only the courage but also the words to say and the wisdom to know what to do. Like God told Joshua, "Be strong and courageous. Do not be frightened, and do not be dismayed, for the LORD your God is with you wherever you go" (Joshua 1:9).

Purity takes a lot of courage. And it wouldn't be called "courage" if you weren't afraid of something. But the more you are drinking deeply from God and His Word, the less you'll be thirsty for things that don't really satisfy–like someone thinking you are cool or staying comfortable when people are making bad choices. Keep being satisfied by God, and you'll be ready to point out a triangle–or a group going the wrong way.

> Blessed is the man who walks not in the counsel of the wicked . . . but his delight is in the law of the LORD, and on his law he meditates day and night. He is like a tree planted by streams of water that yields its fruit in its season, and its leaf does not wither. In all that he does, he prospers. –Psalm 1:1-3

What are things you sometimes "thirst" for that could keep you from doing what is right? How can you meet those thirsts in God or in healthy ways?

Mighty God, I need Your courage. I know I'll need wisdom and help to stand strong even when other people are bent on doing the wrong thing. Help me to trust that You give me everything I need–in life and when I need to stand up for what's right. Let me thirst for You above everything else.

Pure as a Mountain Spring

There once was a quiet forest dweller living high above an Austrian village along the eastern slopes of the Alps. The old gentleman had been hired many years ago by the town council to clear away the debris from the spring that fed the town's water supply. With faithful, silent regularity he patrolled the hills, removed the leaves and branches, and wiped away the silt that would otherwise choke and contaminate the fresh flow of water.

By and by, the village became a popular attraction for vacationers. Graceful swans floated along crystal clear pools. The millwheels of various businesses near the water turned day and night. Farmlands were naturally irrigated. The view from restaurants was picturesque beyond description.

Years passed. One evening the town council met to review the budget. One man's eye caught the salary figure being paid to the obscure keeper of the spring. "Who is this old man? Why do we keep him on year after year? No one ever sees him. He isn't necessary any longer!" By a unanimous vote, they dispensed with the old man's services.

For several weeks nothing changed. By early autumn the trees began to shed their leaves. Small branches snapped off and fell into the pools, hindering the rushing flow of sparkling water. One afternoon someone noticed a slight yellowish-brown tint in the water. A couple days later it was much darker. Within another week, a slimy green film covered sections of the banks, and a foul odor lingered. The millwheels moved more slowly, and some finally ground to a halt. Swans left, as did the tourists. Clammy fingers of disease and sickness reached deeply into the village.

Realizing their gross error in judgment, the embarrassed council called a special meeting. They hired back the old keeper of the spring . . . and within a few weeks the veritable river of life began to clear up. The wheels started to turn, and new life returned to the hamlet in the Alps once again.[1]

Proverbs 4:23 says, "Keep your heart with all vigilance, for from it flow the springs of life." Your heart is much like that river running through the Alpine town. If you don't guard it and care for it, over time it will become contaminated and, trust me, the last thing you want is a slimy green film around your heart.

That old man was doing exactly what you need to do to care for your heart. He was watching out for the smallest little bit of contamination and clearing it out right away. He knew to not let even one small twig collect and build up in that spring. You must have the same vigilance, the same zeal, for caring for your heart. Otherwise, though imperceptible at first, over time the little bits of contamination will build up, and before long your heart will be unrecognizable to yourself, your parents, and your friends.

Since everything in your life flows from your heart, you want to work hard to protect it!

Q. What areas of your heart do you need to do a better job of "keeping" or "guarding"?

Q. What is one specific area of your life that you've noticed a tendency to allow small twigs to build up, where you're neglecting to take care of the little things?

Q. What can you do this week to begin to clean out some of the twigs that have built up in that area of your heart?

---

[1] Peter Marshall and Catherine Marshall, *Mr. Jones, Meet the Master: Sermons and Prayers of Peter Marshall* (New York: Fleming H. Revell, 1951), 147–48. Used by permission.

Mean Girls

There were days when Jesse[1] dreaded going to high school, especially cheerleading practice. That summer, she'd arrived at cheer camp ready to show Christ to her squad. But it was soon clear that something was different from the junior high squad: the whispers while varsity cheerleaders looked at her over their shoulders, the giggles and snide comments in her direction, and the lack of being included on stunts or decision making.

Maybe it was the few extra pounds puberty had layered on or just not having the social skills for high school. Maybe it was her faith—or just the way she was presenting it. But when the doors opened on the first day of school, it didn't feel like a safe place for Jesse.

There was that day when someone said, "Wow! You actually dressed cool today!" Sometimes she'd walk away from a group of popular girls and hear one mimicking something she had said. Her stomach would clench with shame. Fear seized her when certain people passed her in the hall. She felt a stab of jealousy when people admired them. She recalls the cute, popular guy a grade older who made barking noises as she passed him and his friends during lunch hour. "What a dog," he said, laughing.

"That year was so tough," Jesse recalls. She looks down. "In the middle of the year, I found out I needed oral surgery and braces. It was a real struggle between me and God. Here I was, wanting to bring Jesus to my school, and I was a joke to them. Now it felt like God was branding the ridicule right across the middle of my face. It was so hard to understand why He wanted me to suffer like this."

Then Jesse found Isaiah 40:

Why do you say . . . "My way is hidden from the Lord, and my right is disregarded by my God"? Have you not known? Have you not heard? The Lord is the everlasting God, the Creator of the ends of the earth. He does not faint or grow weary; his understanding is unsearchable (verse 27).

"The next verses talk about the strength God gives to the weak," explains Jesse. "I clung to those verses in the midst of a year filled with a lot of fear and shame for me."

And God came through.

"I didn't do everything right. I remember times when I joked about someone else to take the focus off me, or days I resented those cheerleaders," she admits. "But God was very near. And I needed that. I really had to pray about loving my enemies, about how to respond when I wasn't liked. God was just starting to teach me about worshiping Him rather than being consumed with worry over what other people thought."

More than a decade later, Jesse has received some surprising insights into that year. She discovered that one of the cheerleaders' parents soon divorced.

"I wondered what she'd been going through." Jesse shrugs.

But get this . . .

"A lot of the girls on the squad have become Christians!" Jesse marvels. "I don't know if I had something to do with that or not. But two of them have contacted me to tell me they saw Jesus in me. I am incredibly humbled by that–because I know God's power was really being shown in the midst of a very weak time for me. He didn't let me down."

Where shall I go from your Spirit? Or where shall I flee from your presence? If I ascend to heaven, you are there! If I make my bed in Sheol, you are there! –Psalm 139:7–8

---

¹ Not her real name.

Millionaire Next Door

There are some very normal-looking people who have millions of dollars–but you'd never guess it. They drive regular cars, live in regular houses, wear regular clothes, and do regular activities. A lot of them have working-class jobs. But because they have scrimped and saved for decades without the pressure of having to look rich, they've been able to accumulate a great deal of money.

It gets even more interesting. Like many loving parents, they'd like to give their kids the best–better than what they had. Mr. and Mrs. Anonymous Millionaire may invest in a premium education for their kids so they can have more successful jobs, but those jobs may come with an expected image: nice cars, large houses, expensive vacations. You know–all those pricey things their parents, the millionaires-in-disguise, avoided.

But there's more. These parents might give expensive gifts, eliminating the process of self-discipline and other character qualities their kids would gain by earning the cash to purchase those items. Some normal-looking millionaires might help their kids avoid the difficulties of constantly saving and delaying pleasure. And get this: because those kids haven't had to go through the same self-discipline, they may not handle their money in the same wise ways. You see, the challenges in the lives of these parents shaped them so they could handle the rewards of the challenges.[1]

Now, the idea here is not to become a millionaire. But we all have tough things about our lives. Maybe you wish things were different in your family situation, your academic abilities, your relationships at school, or your financial status. Or maybe it's your body–if you could, what would you change about what you see in the mirror and the way it affects your life?

It might be worth wondering what God thinks about that same body. Remember, He's the one who made that stuff you're not so keen on–and He made you in His image as an expression of Himself. He knew why you needed that nose or that body type or those teeth.

The body and face and situations He's given you are picture-perfect for the plans He has written, the people He wants you to connect with, the great story He's written for your life. This isn't to say that we don't need to discipline or take good care of these bodies He's given us; doing this honors Him. But accepting the way He's made us and the situations in which He has placed us is a way of trusting Him. It shows faith in what He has put in place to shape us into the people He needs us to be—for the missions He needs to accomplish. Even the ways people react to your circumstances or appearance prepare you for His plans; they're allowed as *part* of those plans. They can even help you develop compassion, humility, confidence, or other strengths. Like the ordinary-looking millionaires' careful self-discipline, "Suffering produces endurance, and endurance produces character, and character produces hope, and hope does not put us to shame, because God's love has been poured into our hearts" (Romans 5:3-5).

Your circumstances are a part of your story, the character God is creating, and the great adventures He has for you. Rather than wallowing in frustration, seek to "glorify God in your body" (1 Corinthians 6:20). Embrace what He's created as an expression of faith, which is "more precious than gold" (1 Peter 1:7).

I praise you, for I am fearfully and wonderfully made. Wonderful are your works; my soul knows it very well. –Psalm 139:14

[1] Data from Thomas Stanley and William Danko, *The Millionaire Next Door: Surprising Secrets of America's Wealthy* (Dallas: Taylor Publishing, 1996).

One Good Yoke Deserves Another

Do not be unequally yoked with unbelievers. For what partnership has righteousness with lawlessness? Or what fellowship has light with darkness? −2 Corinthians 6:14

What does it mean to be "unequally yoked" with unbelievers? Well, it certainly doesn't mean to avoid mixing chicken eggs with ostrich eggs for breakfast (though you may want to avoid that as well). Nor does it mean to follow a bad "joke" with a good one. No, a yoke is a farming implement used in the days before tractors. It was a piece of wood that sat on top of an animal (like an ox) that enabled the animal to drag things behind it (like a plow).

Often two oxen were yoked together, meaning that they were harnessed together side-by-side. Farmers did this for added power, since two oxen can pull more than one, and also to help each animal stay on track and avoid crazy-shaped rows.

Two oxen work great together, but what if you hooked up an ox to one side of the yoke and your uncle's crazy German shepherd to the other side? How would that work? Being so different in size and temperament, those two animals would be unequally yoked. And that's a problem.

Most likely, the dog, accustomed to being powerful and intimidating, would quickly lose both bark and bite as he was dragged along next to the big ox. And the ox would likely be thoroughly annoyed by a yapping teammate (since most oxen are rather quiet). Even worse, the ox would be slowed by the dog, and the dog would be rubbed in all the wrong places by the yoke.

Before long you'd be plowing in circles without another ox to balance out the yoke. And we're not even talking about how silly this whole arrangement would look to your farmer friends. You'd be laughed right out of the feed store!

Being "unequally yoked" spiritually is a situation you want to avoid as well. You may remember during the Passport2Purity weekend when Dennis Rainey said,

"Don't missionary date." What he means is, don't try to date someone who does not have the same spiritual convictions that you do. Inevitably, the person will distract you from following Christ, slow you down, and have you spinning in circles spiritually. You see, God designed marriage to be a place where two people can get to know Him better. They encourage and help each other stay on track keeping focused on the goal of knowing Christ. And since the purpose of dating is to find a spouse, you want to make sure you are dating someone who shares your spiritual convictions in case you were to marry that person.

Your spiritual life is one of the most intimate and important things a married couple can share. If you are "unequally yoked" then you will never be as close as if you shared the same love for Christ. So make sure your yoke fits whomever you date. And especially make sure to avoid dating a German shepherd.

Q. What are you looking for spiritually in a spouse?

Q. How will you know if someone shares your spiritual convictions?

Q. What kind of questions will you ask them?

Q. Here's a good axiom to follow: "Become the kind of person you want to marry." How can you grow spiritually so you are becoming the kind of person you would want to marry?

DAY TWENTY-TWO
Science and Art

Okay, so this isn't school, but here's a little science lesson you might find interesting.

Let's talk about what happens to a person's brain after sex. (Aha! Got your attention.) Did you know that having sex releases chemicals in your brain? At least two of them.

The first chemical is *dopamine* (sounds like dope-a-mean). It helps us remember the details—whatever our senses experience—of anything that makes us feel good. It's part of our brain's "reward system." It's like putting an invisible tag on something reminding us we want more of whatever it is—pizza, exercise, hugs. We crave more of that tagged item.[1] Dopamine gets into our brains whenever we experience pleasure, but it comes in a really big dose after sex.

The second chemical is *oxytocin* (sounds like ox-ee-toe-sin). This one is basically a bonding chemical. Just after a baby is born and whenever a mom nurses her baby, oxytocin floods her body, and she feels connected to her baby. Sex also dumps a big ol' load of oxytocin into the human body making the person feel very connected to a sexual partner.[2]

See, God did something brilliant when He made sex. It not only feels good, marks our memories vividly, and makes us want more, but it's also like a form of relational superglue.

Now we're moving from science to art. Imagine, if you will, gluing together two different pieces of colored construction paper. After the glue dries, what happens if you try to pull the two sheets apart? You might be able to pull off a few small strips, but neither piece really would stay intact. Because, for the most part, they get stuck together. *Very stuck.*

When the superglue of sex happens in a relationship, it knits a couple together. Sex is powerful stuff. In 1 Corinthians, God says it makes a couple "one flesh" (6:15-19). And one Christian author translates those verses this way, "Your body makes a promise whether you do or not."[3] That is one of the reasons sex is so fantastic in a marriage where a husband and wife are 100 percent committed to each other. Outside of marriage . . . it is still powerful, but in a painful way. The glue starts sticking to things that are very painful to separate and, at times, impossible to forget.

So let's make one lesson out of two. Sex is a powerful glue–either for fantastic purposes or painful ones. God has given you an instruction manual so that it sticks in the ways that are the best for you and the most honoring to Him.

As it is written, "The two will become one flesh." . . . Flee from sexual immorality. Every other sin a person commits is outside the body, but the sexually immoral person sins against his own body. Or do you not know that your body is a temple of the Holy Spirit within you, whom you have from God? You are not your own, for you were bought with a price. So glorify God in your body. –1 Corinthians 6:16, 18–20

What kind of marriage do you want to have someday if it's in God's plan for you to get married? What can you do now that will help make a great relationship later? (For ideas, see Proverbs 31:10–12 and Titus 2:6–8.)

---

[1] http://en.wikipedia.org/wiki/Dopamine.

[2] http://en.wikipedia.org/wiki/Oxytocin.

[3] Lauren F. Winner, *Real Sex: The Naked Truth about Chastity* (Ada, MI: Brazos Press, 2006), 88.

Secret Weapon

Nicole[1] has a great marriage. According to both of them, she and her husband are more in love than ever. They've been married eleven years now, and they have great purpose as they serve God together. Some days, Nicole can hardly believe how good she's got it—and what an incredible husband God had planned for her. She'd been careful about holding off dating until God's timing was right, praying for the guy she would marry, and thinking about what kind of guy she would date—a man who was as passionate about God as she was, who could really lead her toward God, and a man she deeply respected—because she knew God tells wives to respect their husbands (see Ephesians 5:22-33).

Wow, was God ever good.

"I can't believe it," she says as she shakes her head and grins. "My husband's my best friend. I am astounded by the man of God he continues to become. We have so much fun together, and God's adventure for our lives keeps unrolling and amazing us."

But when asked about dating, Nicole reveals one of her secrets.

"I had a secret weapon!" she says, laughing. "One of the best things I did—seriously—was to get my parents involved."

Huh?

"I just realized pretty early on that my parents love God and His Word. They know me, and they've done this dating thing and seen a lot of relationships around them really work, or not. They always seemed to see things I hadn't seen. So figuring it out on my own would have meant missing out," she explains.

"They ended up being my best advisors and even my confidants, you know, as I worked through all the weird boy-girl stuff. It wasn't like they rode in the backseat of the car on dates or anything!" Nicole grins. "I just wanted them involved. A lot of it felt really complicated—with big decisions that could hurt people and affect my life. Even when I got into college I called them and talked to them about different guys."

Nicole's parents took the opportunity to build relationships with the guys in her life, especially those interested in her. She was glad about that.

"The guys became comfortable with my family, which was cool, because my family is obviously really important to me. My parents could talk me through making good decisions about guy stuff because they knew the guys and had seen me with them. I could even watch the guys change, sometimes, as my dad talked with them about spiritual stuff or as they felt accepted. And when I was old enough to get married, it was cool to see the guy who would be my husband really embrace these people I loved so much."

Ephesians 6:1-3 counsels:

Children, obey your parents in the Lord, for this is right. "Honor your father and mother" (this is the first commandment with a promise), "that it may go well with you and that you may live long in the land."

Nicole experienced the reality of this. Obeying your parents and putting yourself under their authority could be something to push against, resist, and get frustrated about. Or, you can choose to honor these people who've been generously and sacrificially caring for you since you were in diapers. You could choose to welcome their insight and authority and use it to help you honor God. Obeying and seeking out your folks' wisdom displays trust in the One who put them in authority, a trust which God is eager to reward.

---

[1] Not her real name.

DAY TWENTY-FOUR
The Egyptian Problem

For this is the will of God, your sanctification: that you abstain from sexual immorality. –1 Thessalonians 4:3

The ancient Egyptians had a problem. Well, actually they had many problems, like walking around in their underwear all the time. But we'll focus on the big one: Pharaoh was considered to be a god to the Egyptians. Now, he wasn't their only god. In fact, they had a long list of gods, but Pharaoh was the only *person* who was also considered a god.

So, guess what? Since he was the only god around to stand up for himself, he made the rules. And this was a problem since the rules kept changing with each new pharaoh. Last year it was, "Sacrifice two pigeons each time you have a bad thought." This year, it's three pigeons. What will it be next year? How do we know when we've made god happy? It's like trying to build a house on shifting sand. (Sound familiar? Read Matthew 7:24-27.)

But here's the good news: You can know what God wants! You can know what makes Him happy; you can know His will. You don't have to guess. He has given us His Word, the Bible, to guide us and let us know what He desires. More than anything, He wants us to commit to following Him and loving Him with our whole heart (see Matthew 22:36-38).

But all through the Bible He also gives us specific instructions. First Thessalonians 4:3 says, "For this is the will of God, your sanctification: that you abstain from sexual immorality." He makes it clear here–no guessing–one way you can please God is to "abstain from sexual immorality." God designed sex, and He designed it to be between a man and woman committed to one another in marriage. "Sexual immorality" is any attempt to undo that definition. It is any thought, word, or action that opposes God's definition of sex.

This is what Jesus addressed in His sermon on lust, "Everyone who looks at a woman with lustful intent has already committed adultery with her in his heart"

(Matthew 5:28). God's will is that you not only avoid having sex until you're married, but that you *think* rightly about sex. This is abstaining from sexual immorality.

Now, who can achieve such a standard? Seem impossible? It is without the indwelling power of the Holy Spirit to guide you. Galatians 5:16 says, "Walk by the Spirit, and you will not carry out the desire of the flesh" (NASB). So how do you walk by the Spirit? By practicing spiritual breathing:[1]

- **Exhale**—Confess your sin; agree with God concerning your sin and thank Him for His forgiveness of it, according to 1 John 1:9 and Hebrews 10:1-25. Confession involves repentance—a change in attitude and action.

- **Inhale**—Surrender the control of your life to Christ and receive the fullness of the Holy Spirit by faith. Trust that He now directs and empowers you, according to the command of Ephesians 5:18 and the promise of 1 John 5:14-15.

Take a moment to identify one way that you may have wrongly viewed God's plan for sex. Practice "abstaining" from sexual immorality by trying the spiritual breathing exercise listed above. First, exhale the sin (confess and repent), and then inhale God's love and forgiveness.

---

[1] Adapted from Bill Bright, *Have You Made the Wonderful Discovery of the Spirit-Filled Life?* (Orlando: NewLife Publications, 1996).

Which Is It?

> **For we are his workmanship, created in Christ Jesus for good works, which God prepared beforehand, that we should walk in them.** –Ephesians 2:10

The question has plagued philosophers for generations. Great scientists have sat scratching their heads. Powerful politicians lie awake at night pondering the answer to this perplexing puzzle. What is this dramatic dilemma?

Which came first–the chicken or the egg?

What? You mean you don't sit around discussing this with friends? Maybe it's not the hot topic it once was (or maybe more people realize it really doesn't matter), but many Christians have asked a similar question, "Which comes first– good works or being a Christian?" To put it another way, do you do good works to *become* a Christian, or do you do good works *because you are a Christian?*

Ephesians 2:10 throws a few eggs in the basket of this argument. It says, "We are his *workmanship, created* in Christ Jesus for *good works,* which God *prepared beforehand,* that we should *walk in them*" (emphasis added).

Here is what those key phrases are saying:

- **Workmanship:** God crafted you; He fashioned you to do something for a reason.

- **Created for good works:** An egg is made for cracking, a chicken is for clucking, and you were created for good works.

- **Prepared beforehand:** Like a cook chopping, slicing, and dicing vegetables and spices, getting all the ingredients ready to go, God made these good works long ago, waiting to be added to the main course (which, in this case, is most likely chicken).

- **Walk in them:** How do you "walk" in works? You live them out. They become part of you, like putting on a pair of shoes with socks soaked in superglue.

You see, God made men and women. And from the very beginning, from the first time He spoke, He had a plan. His plan was that His creations would do good things—things that make Him happy, things that help other people see how good God is. Matthew 5:16 says, "In the same way, let your light shine before others, so that they may see your good works and give glory to your Father who is in heaven."

And they would do these things because they were His children, out of an overflow of their love and relationship with Him. The works are not done to convince God you are good enough to be His child, but because you are His child. The works are a result of being God's creation.

So the next time you crack an egg for breakfast or order a chicken sandwich for lunch, don't worry about which came first, just enjoy your meal. But maybe the food will remind you of Ephesians 2:10 and the reason you were created.

- Ephesians 2:10 is the last verse in a section about God's work on our behalf. Grab a Bible, read verses 1-9, and look for any repeated words that will tell you more about God's work in the passage. (List below)

- What was the state of mankind in verses 1-3?

- What about in verses 4-7?

- What made the difference between the two?

- What "good works" do you sense God calling you to do?